Contents

Introduction

Welcome to Absolute Beginners for Drums.
This book is designed for the complete novice – it will show you everything a beginner needs to know, from setting up your kit for the first time, to how to hold your drumsticks.

Easy-to-follow instructions

will guide you through:
- how to set up your kit
- how to look after it
- how to read rhythmic notation
- classic rock rhythms
- classic fills

Play along with the backing track as you learn – the specially recorded audio will let you hear how the music should sound – then try playing the part yourself.

Practise regularly and often.

Twenty minutes every day is far better than two hours at the weekend with nothing in between.
Not only are you training your brain to understand how to play the drums, you are also teaching your muscles to memorise certain repeated actions.

At the back of this book you will find a section introducing some of the other music available for drums. It will guide you to exactly the kind of music you want to play – you'll soon be able to put your new-found skills to good use with more advanced tutorial books, jazz and blues books, or off-the-record transcriptions.

▼ Queen's **Roger Taylor**

ABSOLUTE BEGINNERS
Drums

To acces audio visit:
www.halleonardmgb.com/mylibrary

6845-5517-1117-7761

HAL•LEONARD®

Published by
Hal Leonard

Exclusive Distributors:
Hal Leonard
7777 West Bluemound Road,
Milwaukee, WI 53213
Email: info@halleonard.com

Hal Leonard Europe Limited
42 Wigmore Street, Marylebone,
London WIU 2 RY
Email: info@halleonardeurope.com

Hal Leonard Australia Pty. Ltd.
4 Lentara Court, Cheltenham,
Victoria 9132, Australia
Email: info@halleonard.com.au

Order No. AM92617
ISBN 0-7119-7429-2
This book © Copyright 1999 by Hal Leonard

Written by Dave Zubraski.
Photographs by George Taylor.
Book design by Chloë Alexander.
Model & drum consultant Jim Benham.

Printed in the EU.

www.halleonard.com

Okay, so after what seems like a lifetime of scheming and planning, you have finally beaten all your opposing relatives and neighbours into submission. There on the floor before you is a mountain of gleaming chrome, wood and plastic – your very first drum kit!

Setting Up Your Kit

Almost every drummer sets their kit up differently. Some choose a basic four- or five-drum kit where others may decide on a more elaborate ten- or twelve-drum kit with a vast array of cymbals and a couple of kitchen sinks. However, every exercise in this book can be played on a basic four-drum kit, which should include the following:

Bass drum, Snare, Top Tom, Floor Tom,
Hi-Hat Stand, Snare Drum Stand, Bass Drum Pedal,
2 Cymbal Stands, 1 Pair of Hi-Hat Cymbals,
1 Ride and 1 Crash Cymbal, as shown below.

Tip

The size of the bass drum will usually determine the sizes of the other drums in the kit. Bass drums can range from 18" to 26", so try to buy a kit that will suit your build. For example, if you are short, a kit with a 20" or 22" bass drum would be more comfortable to play than one with a 24" or 26" bass drum.

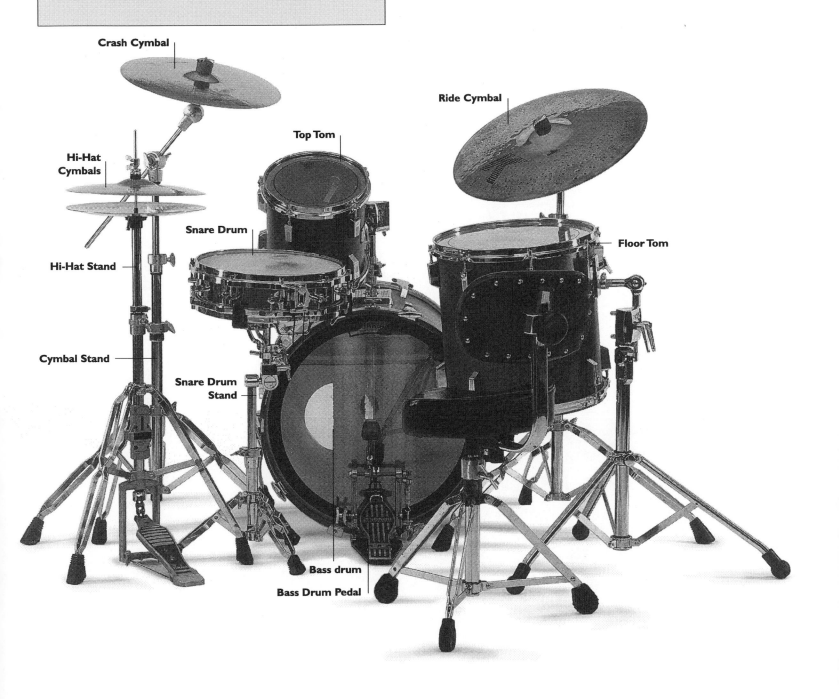

Crash Cymbal

Ride Cymbal

Hi-Hat Cymbals

Top Tom

Hi-Hat Stand

Snare Drum

Floor Tom

Cymbal Stand

Snare Drum Stand

Bass drum

Bass Drum Pedal

Step-by-step guide to setting up

1 Place your bass drum in the centre of where you want the kit to be.

2 Ensure that the front of the bass drum is lifted slightly by adjusting its legs. The "batter head" should be tilted slightly toward where you will be sitting.

4 Now add the top tom (or toms if your kit has more than one). Adjust the tom holder so that the head of the drum is tilted slightly towards the bass drum pedal.

5 Adjust the height of the snare drum so that it is roughly level with your waist. Once again, the head of the drum should be tilted slightly towards you.

7 Place the hi-hat to the left of the snare drum, and adjust the clutch until you can bring the top and bottom cymbals together easily by depressing the pedal.

3 Attach the bass drum pedal to the hoop of the bass drum.

6 Position your floor tom to the right of the bass drum.

9 Make sure that the height of the crash cymbal is adjusted properly – it should be within easy reach.

10 Adjust your stool so that it is at a comfortable height, and make sure that all the drums are within easy reach. Now you're ready to play!

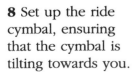

8 Set up the ride cymbal, ensuring that the cymbal is tilting towards you.

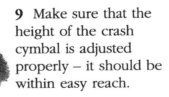

Tuning your drums

Tuning and the choice of drum heads can make a big difference to the overall sound of a drum. Drums are tuned by tightening and loosening the tension rods with a drum key (clockwise tightens, counter-clockwise loosens).

The Snare Drum

When tuning the snare drum, keep both heads quite tight with the snares just taut enough to stop them from rattling. If the snares are adjusted too tight it can stop them vibrating freely, causing them to sound choked. Tune each tension rod in sequence by one turn (as shown in the diagram) until the required sound and feel are obtained.

Tip

The tighter you tune a drum the higher the pitch will become. This also affects the speed of the stick response – the tighter the head the faster the response.

When changing heads choose one that is not too heavy. A very thick head can dull the sensitivity of the snares, which sometimes results in a 'boxy' sound. I would suggest you try a Remo Ambassador head for the batter (top) and a Remo Ambassador snare for the bottom.

Batter Head

Rim (Counter-hoop)

Snare Head (bottom head) and Snares not shown.

Lug

Snare Strainer Throw-off Switch

Snare Tension Adjustment Screw

Tension Rod

Shell

Snare Gate

Tip

Drummer's Jargon: Decay Time

The decay time means how long a note will sound before it dies away. You can alter the decay time as follows: Play one beat on each tom and listen to how long each note rings. Tape a small piece of tissue paper to the top head, away from the area you are playing on to increase the damping, which will decrease the decay time. Adjust all your toms until they have the same decay time.

The Bass Drum

The bass drum is generally tuned as low as possible without losing its tone. To achieve this tighten the heads just enough to take the wrinkles out. A pillow or blanket placed inside against the back head is often used as damping to cut the ring down and produce a good solid "thud".

Tom-Toms

Tom-toms are not usually tuned to any specific note but the smaller sizes are tuned to a higher pitch, getting lower as the sizes get larger. One thing to keep in mind when tuning the toms is to make sure they all have the same decay time.

Posture

When setting up make sure everything is within easy reach.

Sit upright, with a reasonably straight back – don't slouch over the drums or you could end up with a posture like Quasimodo.

Avoid setting the cymbal stands too high or having the toms at angles which are impossible to play.

The top rim of the snare drum should be approximately waist height when you are seated.

The height of your drum stool is also important – go for a position where your thighs are roughly parallel to the floor when you are seated, with your feet resting on the pedals.

Sticks

Bead   **Shoulder**   **Shaft**   **Butt**

Sticks come in many shapes and sizes, so choose a pair that feel comfortable to you. As a suggestion, start with a medium pair of "C" sticks made of hickory wood. Make sure the pair you select are straight and do not resemble bananas! This is easily checked by rolling them on a flat surface – if they wobble it means they are warped, so look for another pair.

Tip

Tap the sticks on the counter and listen to their pitch – try to pick a pair with the same pitch, which means the wood is the same weight and density.

Holding The Sticks
There are two basic ways of holding the sticks:

• the Matched Grip, where both sticks are held in the same way. Most contemporary drummers favour the Matched Grip (for power and speed).

• the Traditional Grip

The Matched Grip – Right Hand

With the palm of your right hand facing towards the floor, hold the stick about one third of the distance from the butt end, so it pivots between the thumb and joint of the first finger. Your thumbnail should point straight down the shaft towards the bead.

The Matched Grip – Left Hand

The left hand grip should be exactly the same as the right hand. Try to keep both hands and fingers as relaxed as possible.

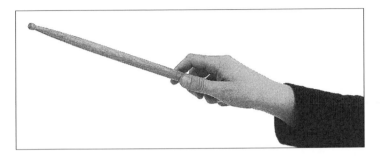

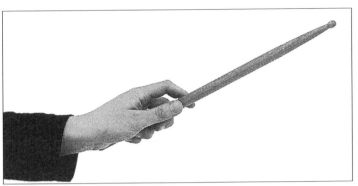

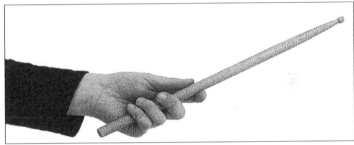

Let your first finger curl around the stick, then bring your second, third and fourth fingers gently around onto the stick to guide and stabilise it. For reference, here is the Traditional Grip. The left hand position is shown below; the right hand position is the same as for the Matched Grip.

Traditional Grip – Left Hand

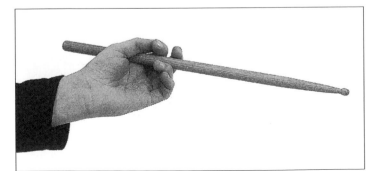

Tip

The left-handed drummer
All the exercises in this book are written assuming that you are right handed; however, if you are left handed play all the exercises with reverse hands and feet.

The stroke

The first step in developing technique is to learn the stroke. Keep your arms fairly steady, moving the sticks mainly from your wrists. Too much arm motion can create a strain in the muscles, hampering your ability to play with speed and control.

1 Hold both sticks about ten inches above the snare drum head. Keep your arms relaxed and slightly away from your body.

2 With a snappy and relaxed motion, drop the bead end of the right stick to the centre of the head and allow it to rebound back to the starting position.

3 Repeat step two with your left stick.

Keep repeating the stroke at a slow but even pace, R L R etc. (R = right hand, L = left hand.)

As you relax you will feel the natural bounce of the stick doing most of the work. Try to obtain the same sound from both sticks.

Tip

For extra practice try starting the stroke with your left hand, (L R L R etc.) making sure that you maintain an even sound from both sticks.

There are two basic ways of playing the bass pedal.

One way is to have the whole foot flat on the pedal.

The other way is to raise the heel of your foot and only use your toes.

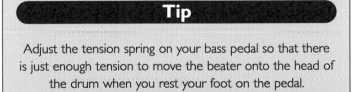

Tip

Adjust the tension spring on your bass pedal so that there is just enough tension to move the beater onto the head of the drum when you rest your foot on the pedal.

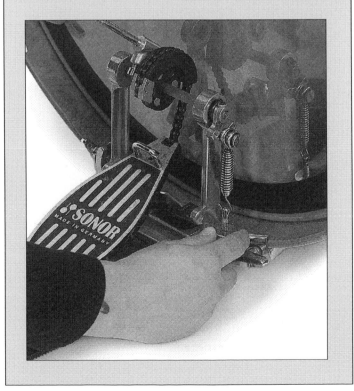

Sometimes a combination of both methods is used. You might find using the toe method is easier for playing faster patterns. I suggest you try both ways to see which is most comfortable for you.

CHECKPOINT

WHAT YOU'VE ACHIEVED SO FAR...

You can now:
• Set up your kit properly
• Tune your drums and adjust decay times
• Hold your sticks correctly
• Use the correct stroke technique
• Use the bass pedal correctly

Reading music

Reading music is easy – once you understand the fundamentals you will take to it in no time.

Drum music is written on five parallel lines called a stave. Each drum is written on a different line within the stave, as shown below.

Cymbal or Hi-Hat
(played with sticks)   Top Tom   Snare   Floor Tom   Bass Drum   Hi-Hat
(played with foot)

When the word "Ride" is written on the cymbal line it means the cymbal pattern is to be played on the ride cymbal. Similarly, when "H.H." is written, the cymbal pattern is to be played on the closed hi-hat (usually with your right hand).

A crash cymbal is shown with a circle around the note. ⊗

In the following example the cymbal rhythm is played on the closed hi-hat with only the first beat played on the crash.

H.H.

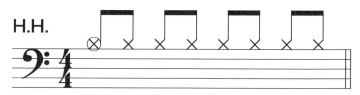

Music has a basic pulse or beat; multiples of these beats are grouped into larger units called bars or measures.

This symbol o is called a semibreve (or whole note) and lasts for the duration of a full bar, so it has a count of four beats. Against the count of **1 – 2 – 3 – 4** you would count semibreves like this:

1 – 2 – 3 – 4 / 1 – 2 – 3 – 4 / 1 – 2 – 3 – 4 / etc

o   o   o

This symbol ♩ is called a crotchet (or quarter note) and lasts for one beat. Thus there are four of these to every bar and they are counted like this:

1 – 2 – 3 – 4 / 1 – 2 – 3 – 4 / 1 – 2 – 3 – 4 / etc
♩ ♩ ♩ ♩ ♩ ♩ ♩ ♩ ♩ ♩ ♩ ♩

The most popular such grouping of beats is known as common time and all the exercises in this book will be in this time (also known as 4/4).

In common time there are 4 evenly placed beats in a bar, which you count:

1 – 2 – 3 – 4 / 1 – 2 – 3 – 4 / 1 – 2 – 3 – 4 / etc

Each time you count "1" you are beginning a new bar. Simple really, isn't it? If you look at any music you can see that notes have different shapes – some have tails, some have solid note heads while others are hollow. Don't worry – they will all soon become very familiar.

This symbol ♩ is called a minim (or half note) and lasts for two beats, so it is counted like this:

1 – 2 – 3 – 4 / 1 – 2 – 3 – 4 / 1 – 2 – 3 – 4 / etc

♩   ♩   ♩   ♩   ♩   ♩

Finally, let's look at a fourth duration, this time for half a beat. This symbol ♪ is called a quaver (or eighth note). There are eight quavers to every bar.

1 & 2 & 3 & 4 & / 1 & 2 & 3 & 4 & / 1 & 2 & 3 & 4 &
♪♪♪♪♪♪♪♪ ♪♪♪♪♪♪♪♪ ♪♪♪♪♪♪♪♪

To count quavers we subdivide each beat into two parts and they are counted like this:

1 & 2 & 3 & 4 &, etc

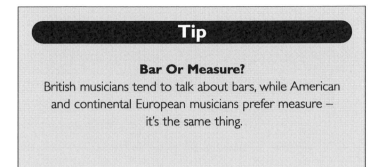

Now let's put theory into practice and play along with the band!

Join the band

In the first example you will need to concentrate on counting. As **Track 1** is written in common time (or 4/4), you will hear a four beat count at the start. Keep the hi-hat closed with your left foot on the pedal and play the crotchet (quarter note) closed hi-hat pattern with your right hand.

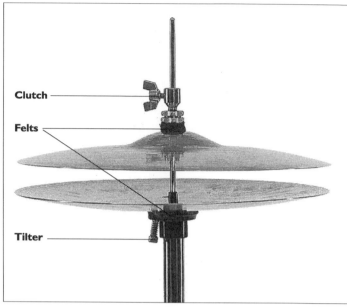

H.H.

Count 1, 2, 3, 4 throughout the track, making sure that each count coincides exactly with each strike of the hi-hat. If you get out of time with the music, stop and start again from the beginning.

Tip

For extra practice start anywhere in Track 1 and try to pick up the count as before: 1, 2, 3, 4 etc.

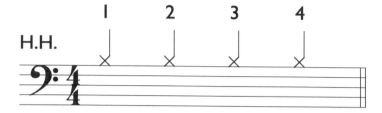

Keeping good time means not speeding up or slowing down. This is especially important for the drummer. You may have greatest rhythms and fills in the world, but if you can't play in time you will never be popular with your fellow musicians.

To develop a good sense of time, practise all the exercises with the audio tracks and with a metronome. Try playing each exercise at different tempos, from slow to fast.

Never speed up or slow down gradually (unless specified) – keep a steady beat throughout. Always take a short break before trying an exercise at a new tempo.

Tip

Keep Listening!
Whenever you're listening to the radio or a CD try counting to the music. You may think this is simple to do, but you will be teaching yourself the discipline of counting and playing in time. Learning to count regular beats is something that comes as second nature to most musicians, but this is only because they have worked hard at it in the early stages.

CHECKPOINT

WHAT YOU'VE ACHIEVED SO FAR...

You can now:
• Read basic drum notation
• Understand simple note values
• Play your first drum pattern

Basic rock rhythms

Now let's try playing a basic rock rhythm. We'll break it down into three stages:

Stage 1 Play the following quaver (or eighth note) rhythm on the closed hi-hat with your right hand.

Say the count as you play: **1** & **2** & **3** & **4** & etc.

Keep practising this exercise until you can play it with smoothness and ease.

Track 2 demonstrates this rhythm slowly, and

Track 3 speeds it up a bit.

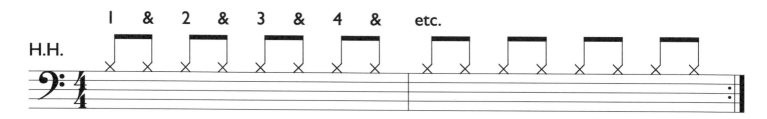

Stage 2 Play the hi-hat rhythm as before, but now also play the snare drum with your left hand on beats 2 and 4. This means that on beats 2 and 4 you are playing both the snare and hi-hat simultaneously.

Track 4 is a slower example of this rhythm.

If you have trouble putting the snare and hi-hat parts together, isolate the snare part and just play on beats 2 & 4. Once you've got that rock steady, add the quaver hi-hat part.

Track 5 is slightly faster.

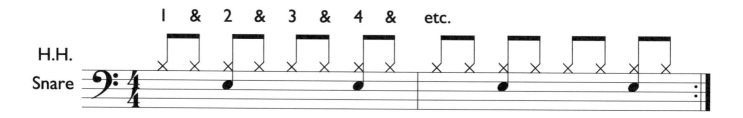

Tip

This symbol 𝄇 is called a repeat sign and it means you play all the bars that fall between two such signs twice. The first repeat sign is usually left out if it comes at the beginning of a piece.

When playing the closed hi-hat and snare drum your right hand crosses over your left hand as shown in the photograph.

Stage 3 Play the bass drum with your right foot on beats 1 and 3. When playing the bass and snare parts, make sure every beat falls exactly in time with the hi-hat pattern. And don't forget to keep counting!

Listen to **Track 6** to hear how this should sound.

Once you're feeling confident, try playing along with **Track 7**, which is a little faster.

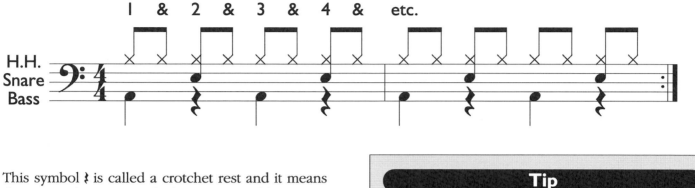

This symbol ⃰ is called a crotchet rest and it means these are silent notes which are counted but not played, so only play the bass drum on beats 1 and 3 as shown.

Tip

Sound and Silence

Rests are vitally important to all musicians – especially drummers! In fact, what you don't play is just as important as what you do play – so count rests just as carefully as any other note.

Play with the band

Having practised the basic rock rhythm on its own, let's have some fun and try using it with the band.

Have a look through the example below, which lasts for nine bars. The first four bars are repeated; this equals eight counts of four, then in the ninth bar you'll end on a crash cymbal and bass drum on beat 1.

Many rhythms demonstrated in this book have been used on lots of great records – this particular rhythm is a rock standard and has been used by artists as diverse as Oasis and The Rolling Stones. As you become familiar with different patterns you will be able to recognise and appreciate the parts played by other drummers.

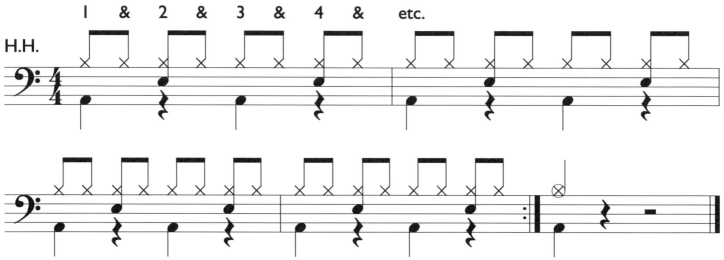

On **Track 8** there is a full band with drums – have a listen and count along with the drum part.

Track 9 is the band minus drums – this is your chance to step in and take over the drummer's stool. Don't forget that all tracks start with a four-beat count-in.

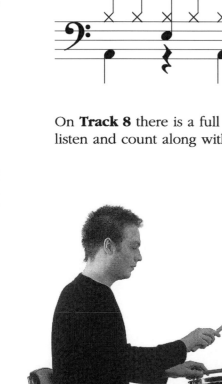

CHECKPOINT

WHAT YOU'VE ACHIEVED SO FAR...

You can now:

• Play a complete rock drum rhythm
• Co-ordinate bass, snare and hi-hat parts
• Play along with a full band backing track

Now you have gained some co-ordination between your hands and feet, let's try some rhythms using different bass drums patterns.

This example is another classic rock rhythm using a crotchet (quarter note) and quaver (eighth note) bass drum pattern. Start by isolating the bass drum pattern – practise it until it almost becomes automatic. Then add the snare drum part, and finally, add the quaver hi-hat part. Make sure the hi-hat pattern remains constant in both volume and tempo.

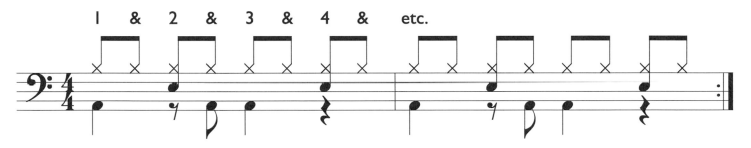

Note the quaver bass drum rest ⁊ on beat 2. As with all rests these beats are counted but not played. Listen to **Track 10**, and then try playing along.

Once you've mastered that, try playing along with **Track 11**, which is a little faster.

In the next example, we'll take the same classic rock rhythm and add another bass drum variation. Listen to **Track 12**, and try and pick out the bass drum rhythm, then practise that part on its own. Make sure you've got that part absolutely steady before you attempt to add the snare part.

Finally, make sure every bass drum beat falls exactly in time with the hi-hat pattern.

Track 13 is a faster rendition of this rhythm.

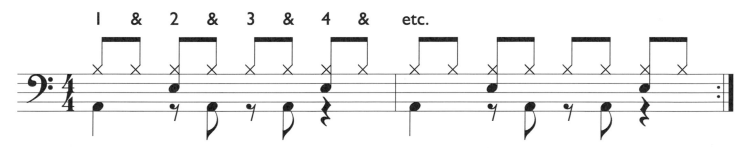

Metallica's **Lars Ulrich**

The rhythm section

One of the most enjoyable aspects of playing drums is playing with other musicians and making music. In every band it is important that the bass and drums form a solid groove for the other musicians to play or sing over – in fact they are often referred to collectively as the rhythm section. To achieve this your bass drum pattern should closely follow the notes being played by the bass guitar, or vice versa.

This next example takes the rhythm you have just been practising and shows how the bass and drums can work together – listen to **Track 14** to hear how the bass drum pattern locks in with the bass guitar.

▲ **Keith Moon** of The Who – a classic rock drummer

Track 15 has the drum part removed, so that you can play along.

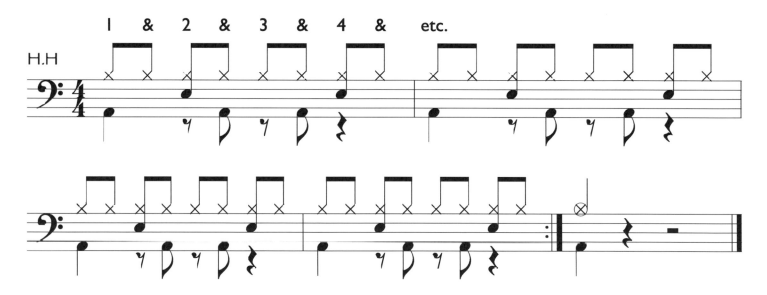

CHECKPOINT

WHAT YOU'VE ACHIEVED SO FAR...

You can now:
• Play two classic rock rhythms with different bass drum parts
• Play along with a full band, and "lock in" with the bass part

So far you've only played rhythms where the snare drum plays on beats 2 and 4. In the next example the snare falls on beat 2 and on the "& 4 &". The hi-hat and bass drum play the same pattern throughout. Practise the bass and snare parts together and then add the hi-hat part.

Track 16 gives you the rhythm played slowly.

Track 17 speeds it up.

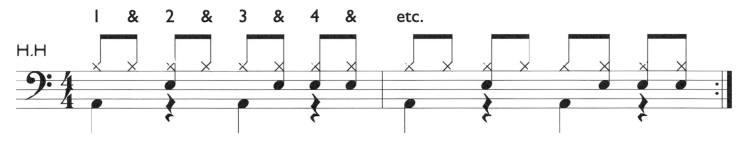

Here's another variation on the same basic rhythm, with a different snare pattern. Once again, practise the bass and snare part together, and then add the hi-hat, making sure that the snare drum beats fall exactly in time with the hi-hat pattern.

Practise slowly along with **Track 18** –

try **Track 19** once you're a little more confident.

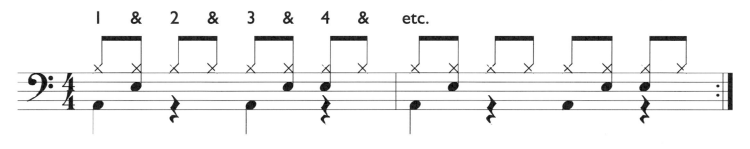

The crash cymbal

The crash cymbal is often used to highlight the beginning of a phrase or accent certain musical figures. To play the crash, strike the edge of the cymbal with the shoulder or shaft of the drum stick, using your normal grip.

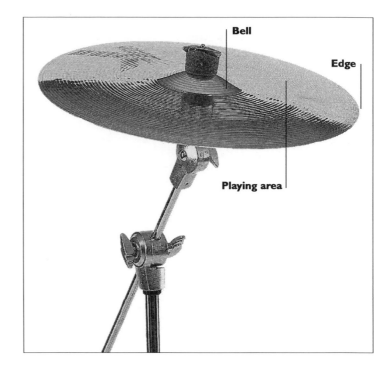

Here's a track with the band that will give you a chance to try out that crash!

Check out this repeated four-bar phrase, which features the crash cymbal on beat one of bars 1, 5 and 9 – listen to **Track 20** to hear the full band version.

Note also that in the fourth and eighth bars the snare drum plays a slightly different pattern.
Don't forget to keep counting as you play!

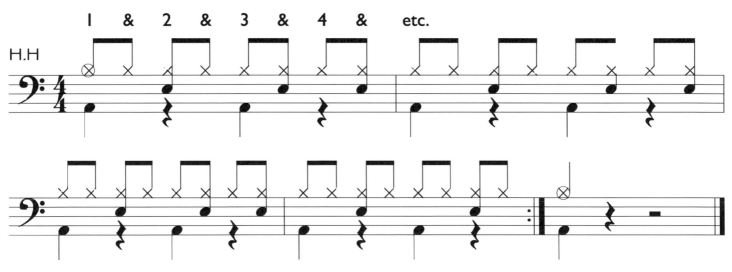

Track 21 is your chance to play along with the rest of the band.

CHECKPOINT

WHAT YOU'VE ACHIEVED SO FAR...

You can now:
- Play two more classic rock rhythms with different snare drum parts
- Use your crash cymbal

Tip

When practising these rhythms for the first time try breaking them down by playing the closed hi-hat and snare drum part first, then the hi-hat and bass drum part. Finally, bring both of them together to form the complete exercise.

So far we have looked at rhythms using different bass and snare drum patterns in separate exercises, but now we will combine these ideas to form more interesting rhythms.

By using this mix-and-match approach to your drumming you can increase the patterns available to you. Don't be afraid to experiment – create some patterns of your own!

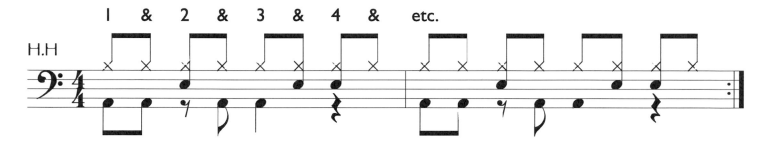

Track 22 – slow version   **Track 23** – faster version

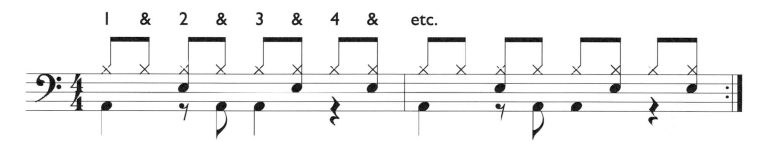

Track 24 – slow version   **Track 25** – faster version

Now let's join the band again – this time you're going to play a rhythm with an interesting snare and bass drum pattern that works well with the parts played by other members of the band.

Listen to the full band version on **Track 26**,

and then try playing along with **Track 27**.

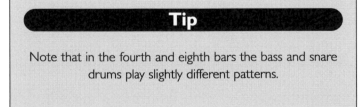

Tip

Note that in the fourth and eighth bars the bass and snare drums play slightly different patterns.

CHECKPOINT

WHAT YOU'VE ACHIEVED SO FAR...

You can now:
• Combine different snare and bass drum patterns

In order to explore drum fills we need to introduce another note called a semiquaver (or sixteenth note). It looks similar to the quaver but has two tails instead of one ♪.

When playing in common time (4/4) there are sixteen semiquavers to every bar. To count semiquavers we subdivide each beat into four parts and they are counted like this:

1 e & a, 2 e & a, 3 e & a, 4 e & a etc
♪ ♪ ♪ ♪ ♪ ♪ ♪ ♪ ♪ ♪ ♪ ♪ ♪ ♪ ♪ ♪

Here's your first chance to try some semiquavers. Count steadily as you play and make sure each count coincides with each beat played. Start with both sticks at the same height above the drum and play this exercise using the technique as described in the stroke on page 14.

Track 28 lets you hear how it should sound.

Double Stroke Sticking
In all the exercises so far you have been playing one beat with each hand – this is known as single stroke sticking: R L R L etc. For extra practice, you can play this exercise using double stroke sticking – playing two beats with each hand: R R L L etc.

Now add the bass drum and hi-hat parts to form the rhythm written out below. You will notice the bass drum falls on beats **1**, **2**, **3**, **4** throughout, with the hi-hat falling on beats **2** and **4**.

The hi-hat part is written out at the bottom of the stave, because instead of hitting it with your right hand, as you have been doing up to now, you're going to open and close it with your left foot on the hi-hat pedal.

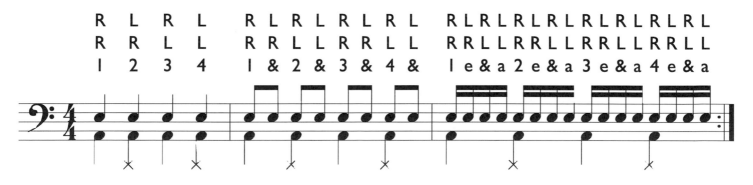

For extra practise play this exercise using double stroke sticking (as shown above the stave).

Make sure your bass drum maintains a constant tempo while the snare part doubles up each bar, playing 4, 8, then 16 beats.

Listen to **Track 29**, and practise slowly until you can play along.

Setting up the hi-hat

When setting up your hi-hat, position the bottom cymbal six to ten inches above the top rim of the snare.

Adjust the clutch to secure the top cymbal so that the felts touch the cymbal without choking it.

Position the cymbals so that they are 1/2" to 1 1/2" apart. Finally, adjust the bottom cymbal tilter to give the cymbal a slight tilt.

Tip

Drum fills are generally used when moving from one section of a song to another. When you play a drum fill it is important to keep the tempo and groove rock steady.

Clutch

Felts

Tilter

When playing the ride cymbal, strike the cymbal with the bead of the stick, about halfway between the bell and the outer edge.
Let the stick rebound after every beat.

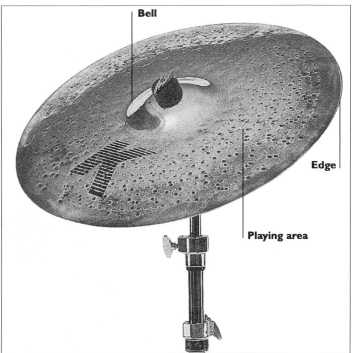

The next example contains two contrasting bars:

In bar 1 use your right hand to play the cymbal pattern on the ride cymbal and your left foot to close the hi-hat on beats **2** and **4** (simultaneously with the snare).

In bar 2 play a bar of semiquavers on the snare drum, maintaining a steady beat throughout the bar with the bass drum and hi-hat.

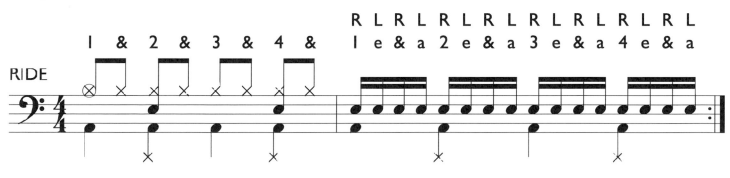

Listen to **Track 30** to hear how this should sound, and then try playing along.

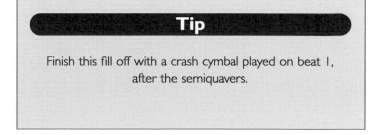

Tip

Finish this fill off with a crash cymbal played on beat 1, after the semiquavers.

A classic rock fill

Here's another variation on the one bar drum fill you've just learnt. The fourth semiquaver note of each group of four has been replaced by a quaver note on the "&", which is equal to two semiquaver notes. The first bar is the same as in the previous example.

Track 31 demonstrates how this fill should sound.

The Rolling Stones'
Charlie Watts

Led Zeppelin's
John Bonham

CHECKPOINT

WHAT YOU'VE ACHIEVED SO FAR...

You can now:

- Use the hi-hat pedal
- Use the ride cymbal
- Experiment with double stroke sticking
- Play your first fills

The Grand Finale

Now you have the chance to play a complete drum part, complete with fills, along with a full backing band. You'll have a chance to use all of the new skills you've developed.

In the example on the next page, the music has been written in four-bar sections – the fills are played on every fourth bar. In fact, if you listen to your favourite songs and count the numbers of bars, you'll find that fills nearly always occur at intervals of 4, 8 or 16 bars – because that's the way pop music is constructed.

The fill lasts one beat and starts on beat 4. Often a simple but effective one- or two-beat fill will flow better than a fill over a whole bar or more.

Listen to **Track 32** and follow your drum part – then have a go yourself with the full band on **Track 33**.

Tip

Note that the cymbal pattern changes from the closed hi-hat to the ride (or vice versa) after every fill.

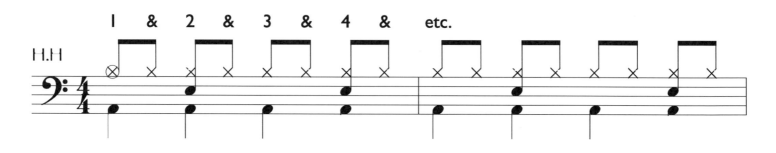

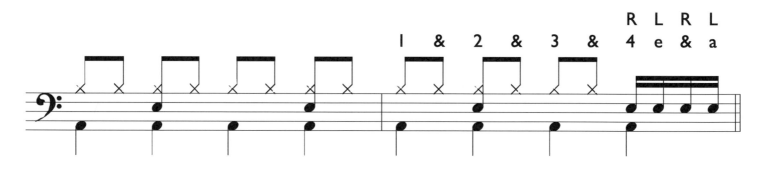

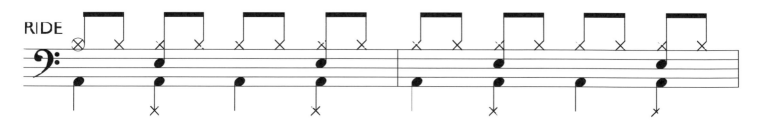

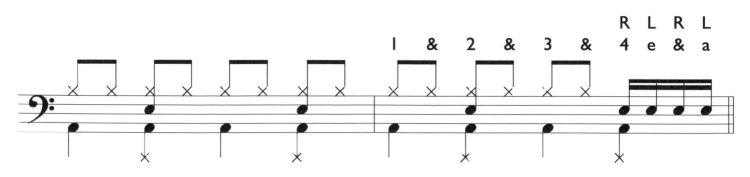

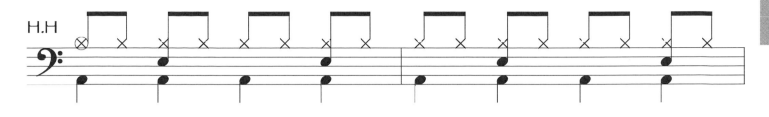

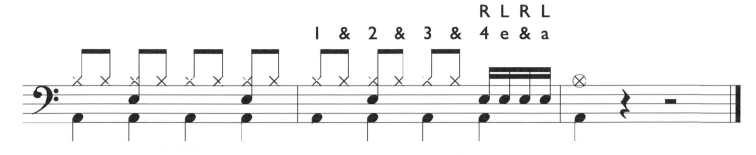

R L R L

1 & 2 & 3 & 4 e & a

H.H

CHECKPOINT

WHAT YOU'VE ACHIEVED SO FAR...

Congratulations! You've now reached the end of the instructional part of this book.

You can now:
• Co-ordinate your bass drum, snare, hi-hat, crash and ride cymbals
• Play in time along with the backing tracks
• Play classic rock rhythms including fills

Care and maintenance

A well-maintained kit will last longer, look better, and, more importantly, be less likely to let you down at a gig or recording session.

1 Keep all tension rods, screws, springs, snare release etc. lightly oiled.

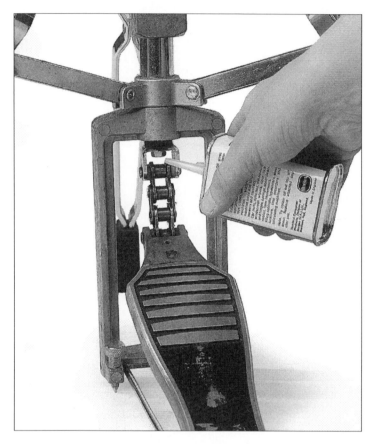

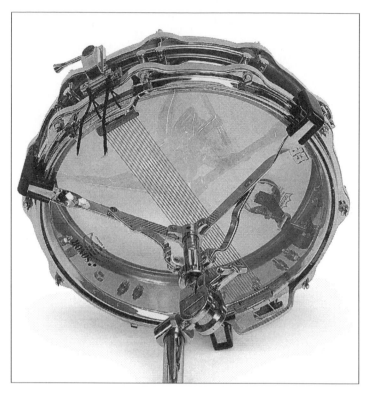

2 Snares are the most delicate part of the drum kit, so try not to touch them unnecessarily, and do not lay anything on top of them as this can cause the thin strands of wire to bend. If this happens they will vibrate unevenly causing an annoying buzz.

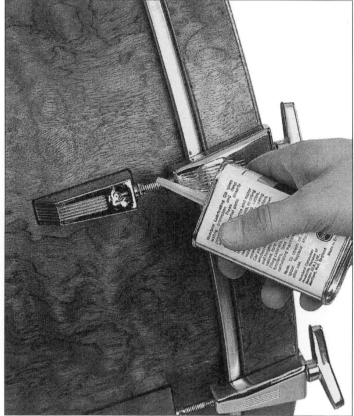

3 Cymbals can be cleaned (not too often) with cymbal cleaner (obtained at most music stores) or washed with warm soapy water using a sponge.

Make sure you dry the cymbal completely after washing.

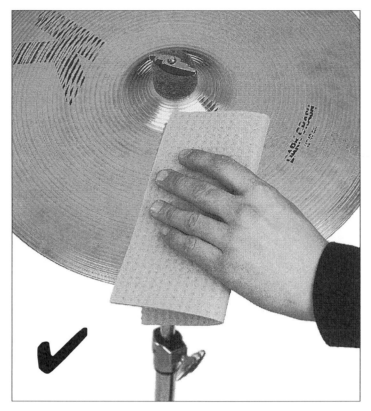

Be careful not to use anything abrasive, such as metal cleaner, scouring pad etc. as this can cause damage to a cymbal.

Do not clamp your cymbals to the stands too tightly, as this can prevent them from vibrating freely and may possibly cause them to crack.

4 If the chrome parts on your kit get very dirty you can clean them with a light grade of wire wool. Dip the wool in some oil first, then gently clean the dirt or rust away.

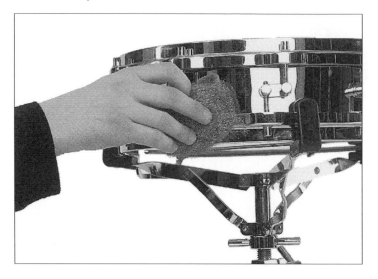

5 When transporting your kit a set of waterproof fibre cases is recommended. These come in all different sizes so make sure you know the measurements of your drums before buying them.

6 Most drum heads are made of plastic and are very durable. However, with constant use they will gradually lose their tone and become less responsive and should be replaced.

7 Do not store your drums too near a heat source such as a radiator, open fire etc.

Armed with the basic drumming techniques you've learnt in this book, you should now be able to work out some of the drum parts to classic songs. Listen to some of the following great drum parts and try to figure out what the drummer is doing!

Be My Baby The Ronettes
Fifty Ways To Leave Your Lover Paul Simon
Green Onions Booker T & The MGs

Honky Tonk Woman The Rolling Stones
I Am The Resurrection The Stone Roses
I Can't Explain The Who
Rain The Beatles
Tomorrow Never Knows The Beatles
Voodoo Chile Jimi Hendrix
We Will Rock You Queen
When The Levee Breaks Led Zeppelin
White Room Cream

Cozy Powell – a legend of rock drumming

other drum books you might like

AM994015

AM1010130

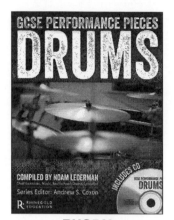

RHG540

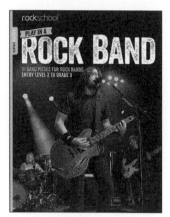

RSK071402

RSK041406R

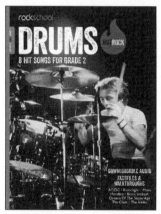

RSK041407R

RSK041408R

RSK051220

AM1000406R

AM979869

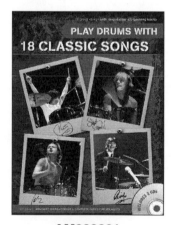

AM999361

Just visit your local music shop and ask to see our
huge range of music in print.

www.halleonard.com